FIND TIME TO WRITE

A BEGINNER'S GUIDE TO THE WRITING HABIT

LOUISE TONDEUR

D1519023

WWW.SMALLSTEPSGUIDE.CO.UK

WHY YOU SHOULD READ THIS BOOK

Is this book for me?
You are in the right place if you want to:

- establish a writing habit for the first time
- schedule regular writing time for a longer writing project
- get your hands on a bunch of writing prompts

Small steps in a nutshell
Find Time to Write, and all the other books in the series, are based on the Small Steps Method. You can take a task, however daunting, and break it down into smaller and smaller steps. You can do small, specific things in your everyday life towards achieving your goals. In other words, you can start taking small steps today and end up with a writing habit in 30 days time. Are you up for the challenge?

Free goodies, just for you
Take a look at the videos that accompany this book at:

www.louisetondeur.co.uk/find-time-to-write-book/free-video-series-find-time-to-write/

I'm not going to advise you to do anything I wouldn't do myself. I'm writing my third novel at the moment and you can find out how it's going by joining my author mailing list. You'll get a freebie in return - usually a free story or cheatsheet: www.louisetondeur.co.uk

You are welcome to download a free chapter from my book on the Small Steps Method here: www.smallstepsguide.co.uk/books

INTRODUCTION

Welcome

This book challenges you to schedule your writing time over the next few weeks, 15 minutes at time, or for half an hour, an hour, or two hours if you can manage it. Your call.

How to use this book

The book is in two sections: 'Beginnings' and 'Your Thirty Day Writing Challenge'. 'Your Thirty Day Writing Challenge' is where the main action is. Go ahead and skip straight to it if you like. You've got a couple of alternatives:

1. Start with 'Beginnings' if you do not write yet, or you are a beginner. This section eases you into a writing habit over three weeks.
2. If you already write, skip the three week set up, but it's worth scanning this section and circling the exercises that appeal to you so you get to check them out later.
3. Write down *when and where you write* and *what your energy level was like*. Simply take a few seconds to

add this to the end of your writing in your notebook or computer each time. For instance: at the Sunshine Café, 11-11.30am, feeling tired.

About writing every day

OK, time to contradict myself: you don't actually have to write every day for these exercises to work. The key thing is that you schedule your writing time. If you need to take 60 days to do the writing challenge, no problem – as long as you *schedule*. If you can't manage to write every day, create another kind of habit - three days a week, or every Saturday morning, or every Thursday evening. The exercises still work. Before you start, adapt the challenge to fit your schedule. Spend half an hour scheduling your writing time today.

PART I
BEGINNINGS: THREE
WEEKS TO A WRITING
HABIT

BEGINNINGS: AN INTRODUCTION

*T*he beginnings section is designed to help you make a habit out of your writing. Here are some tips:

Set the alarm 15 minutes earlier OR make yourself a packed breakfast the night before and leave the house 15 minutes earlier so you can write on the bus / train OR write while the kids fall asleep, with a glass of something. Do this for at least three days in a row to kick-start the habit.

In this section you get a different writing prompt each day for three weeks. These are designed to slot into your day. Carry this workbook with you.

Day seven is a day off. Don't skip it. It's important to take time off. Plus, like leaving mulled wine to mull or bread to rise, your mind needs to work on your creative ideas. By 'take the day off' I mean have a day off from writing. You may not be able to take a whole day off to relax – although that would be good too - but try to spend half an hour at least doing something nice for yourself. It doesn't have to be day seven – pick a day that works for you.

If you're already writing and these exercises don't feel

challenging enough create the habit anyway. You can write anything. Your challenge is to schedule the time to write regularly and to try writing in different environments.

Remember to jot down *when and where you write* and *what your energy level was like* at the end of each writing session.

BEGINNINGS WEEK ONE

*W*rite for 15 minutes every day for a week. Use the prompts in this section to kick-start your writing. This page is for notes.

DAY ONE

As you go about your daily life, observe the things and places around you. Observe the people, the way they move and talk.

DAY TWO

Go and sit in a café and observe the world around you, including the people.

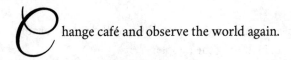

Change café and observe the world again.

DAY FOUR

G o for a walk round the block, noticing the details. Notice people, sounds, textures and colours.

DAY FIVE

Sit for a while in a train station, observing objects, sounds, ephemera, weather, and watching people come and go.

DAY SIX

*S*pend some time in a park or a museum, watching the world around you. Notice in particular the small details.

DAY SEVEN

*H*ave a day off. Do something nice for yourself. Record what you did on this page – but do that tomorrow.

BEGINNINGS WEEK TWO

rite for 15 minutes every day for a week. Use the prompts in this section to kick-start your writing. This page is for notes.

DAYS ONE AND TWO

Freewriting. Start with a colour. Write for 5 minutes without stopping. Repeat.

DAYS ONE AND TWO

*F*reewriting. Start with a colour. Write for 5 minutes without stopping. Repeat.

DAYS THREE AND FOUR

*S*enses. Right where you are now, what can you see, hear, smell, taste, touch? Write a line about each one.

DAYS THREE AND FOUR

*S*enses. Right where you are now, what can you see, hear, smell, taste, touch? Write a line about each one.

DAY FIVE

*D*oorway. Write about the nearest doorway to you right now. Use all of your senses.

DAY SIX

Object. Pick up an object near you and observe it for 5 minutes. Write about it.

DAY SEVEN

*H*ave a day off. Do something nice for yourself. Record what you did on this page – but do that tomorrow.

BEGINNINGS WEEK THREE

*W*rite for 15 minutes every day for a week. Use the prompts in this section to kick-start your writing. This page is for notes.

DAY ONE

Combine three people you have observed in real life into one made-up person.

DAY TWO

*W*rite a description of a stranger.

DAY THREE

Describe a made-up person, focusing entirely on how he or she moves.

DAY FOUR

*D*escribe a made-up person, focusing entirely on how he or she talks.

DAY FIVE

The people from days 3 and 4 meet up.

DAY SIX

*C*reate a place: a park, a hospital, a school or a hotel. Write it as if you were the person from day three.

DAY SEVEN

*H*ave a day off. Do something nice for yourself. Record what you did on this page – but do that tomorrow.

PART II
YOUR 30 DAY WRITING CHALLENGE

INTRODUCTION TO YOUR 30 DAY WRITING CHALLENGE

*H*ow it works

You get a series of writing prompts to respond to over thirty days. These are all designed to help you get into the habit of writing regularly. Write straight into this workbook, and carry it around with you so you don't forget. In week one the writing prompts are pretty straight-forward. As the thirty day challenge progresses, the writing tasks get more involved. They are designed to build one on the other. Some of the writing tasks involve leaving the house. If you can't leave the house, leave the house in your imagination. By the way, if you are into tech tools, you might also want to use an App called Evernote to capture ideas.

Important: Remember to jot down *when and where you write* and *what your energy level was like* at the end of each writing session. Over the 30 Day Challenge a pattern should start to emerge! You get to review what happened at the end of the month.

YOUR 30 DAY WRITING CHALLENGE: WEEK ONE

*W*hat to do during week one
The writing tasks in the first week are nice and accessible. (If they're too easy, double up the activities by picking and choosing from the beginnings section.) This is because the big challenge, in the first week, is tracking your time. The first week also involves writing in different places at different times. This is so you get a sense of when's best for you. Go with it. If you can't change time / place every day in the first week try to incorporate this strategy as you go along, and remember, if you can't write every day, adapt and set up your own writing timetable in advance.

TRACK YOUR TIME

During the first week, I want you to track your time. Every couple of hours – or at meal times – write down what you've been doing with your time.

DAY ONE

*L*ATE IN THE DAY: Starting with the word BLUE, write a list of words. Play word association with yourself. No other rules! Afterwards, jot down a couple of words about how you felt writing at this time of day: energetic, enthusiastic, tired, overwhelmed, happy, for instance.

DAY TWO

*E*ARLY IN THE MORNING: Starting with the word TREE, write a list of words. Play word association with yourself. Afterwards, jot down how you felt writing at this time of day.

DAY THREE

MID-MORNING: go somewhere and write a list of words about the place you are in. Afterwards, jot down a couple of words about how you felt writing at this time of day.

DAY FOUR

*L*UNCHTIME: go to your favourite café and write what you can see. Make your list of words. Afterwards, jot down a couple of words about how you felt writing at this time of day.

DAY FIVE

MID-AFTERNOON: Write a list of what you see in your home or at your desk at work. Afterwards, jot down a couple of words about how you felt writing at this time of day.

DAY SIX

*R*eview your week: review what you wrote, and your time tracking. How are you spending your time? Did anything surprise you?

DAY SEVEN

*H*ave a day off. Do something nice for yourself. Record what you did on this page – but do that tomorrow.

YOUR 30 DAY WRITING CHALLENGE: WEEK TWO

What to do during week two

Week two focuses on getting over one of the main barriers to writing: thinking you have to come up with an idea first. You don't. Trust these writing prompts and give them ago. If you can't think of anything else to write, make lists about what you can see.

DAY EIGHT

*W*rite for a minute without stopping. Set a timer. Try five minutes, then ten minutes. What you write doesn't have to make sense. The only rule is: keep writing!

DAY NINE

*W*atch something for a minute. Set a timer. Now try five minutes. What about ten minutes? Don't write, simply observe. Write a list of words based on what you observed.

DAY TEN

*G*o out somewhere to write: a museum, art gallery, or park. Take this workbook with you. Jot down your sense impressions. You can write lists or sentences.

DAY ELEVEN

*S*it in a café and write a story about someone in a café in another part of the world. Make it somewhere you've visited.

DAY TWELVE

*R*eview what you've written so far. Note anything you want to continue or that sparks off a story or poem or blog post.

DAY THIRTEEN

ou need a friend for this one, preferably someone who lives somewhere else. Look out of a window or doorway three times, at different times of the day and write about it. As you do, deliberately go through each of your senses. Get a friend to do the same, at the same time, wherever they are in the world. Share the results with one another. Email is probably the easiest way to share the work.

Optional extra: repeat this a few times with different people and share the results with each other.

DAY FOURTEEN

*H*ave a day off. Do something nice for yourself. Record what you did on this page – but do that tomorrow.

YOUR 30 DAY WRITING CHALLENGE: WEEK THREE

*W*hat to do during week three

Week three challenges your imagination using physical prompts – the kind that most people would pass by. You're going to look for ephemera, postcards, photographs and other found objects.

Try to think about the provenance of the ephemera, post-card or found object find. Where has it come from and who has owned it? Who made it? Who used it? Imagine a history for it.

DAYS FIFTEEN AND SIXTEEN

*C*ollect together three pieces of ephemera. Write about them. Now find an everyday object from the past in a museum, local shop, or a relative's house. Who used it?

NB days fifteen and sixteen are the same to allow you time to do this.

DAYS FIFTEEN AND SIXTEEN

*C*ollect together three pieces of ephemera. Write about them. Now find an everyday object from the past in a museum, local shop, or a relative's house. Who used it?

NB days fifteen and sixteen are the same to allow you time to do this.

DAY SEVENTEEN

*B*uy a postcard. Write it as if you were a made up character.

DAY EIGHTEEN

*S*earch in junk shops, car boot sales or online for old postcards. Write about the people who sent and received them.

DAY NINETEEN

*E*xamine some old photographs. What happened next?

DAY TWENTY

*I*magine you are one of the people in the photographs you looked at. Write a postcard as if you are that person.

DAY TWENTY-ONE

*H*ave a day off. Do something nice for yourself. Record what you did on this page – but do that tomorrow.

YOUR 30 DAY WRITING CHALLENGE: WEEK FOUR

hat to do during week four
Week four is all about people. It uses fictional people and real people to give you a sense of what it is like to write both fiction and memoir. You will need to do a bit of preparation as day twenty-three requires you to interview someone. The writing prompts in week four are more involved than in previous weeks, too. For instance, day twenty-seven involves working on a play – so you also get a taste of more than one genre this week.

DAY TWENTY-TWO

*I*magine you are one of the people who used the objects from the past you looked at on day twenty. Write down a memory, as if you were that person.

DAY TWENTY-THREE

*I*nterview people in your family or one of your friends' families. Talk with a senior citizen and jot down some impressions of what they said afterwards. Do the same with a young child and with a teenager.

DAY TWENTY-FOUR

*D*raw a family tree for your immediate family or create one that describes your friendship group. Go back a couple of generations if you can. Fictionalise one of the people on the outer branches of the tree - someone you don't know.

DAY TWENTY-FIVE

*D*escribe a memory you can recall from childhood. Try to use something fairly mundane and everyday, and include small details if you can.

DAY TWENTY-SIX

*T*here are two parts to today's challenge.

1. Can you imagine yourself as older than you are?
   Again use an everyday scene. Try visualising it and
   describing it.
2. Imagine an old person's face, with many lines.
   Describe his or her face and find images to
   describe the lines and the places where the person
   may have been.

DAY TWENTY-SEVEN

What are your neighbours like? Write about a fictional neighbour, focusing on facial expressions and body language. Get them to speak to another fictional neighbour. Write the beginning of a play. Bring your two characters on stage and have them speak about the weather.

Get some friends together. Get them to speak your play out loud, and act it out if possible.

DAY TWENTY-EIGHT

*H*ave a day off. Do something nice for yourself. Record what you did on this page – but do that tomorrow.

YOUR 30 DAY WRITING CHALLENGE: WEEK FIVE

hat to do during week five
        Week five is about reviewing and consolidating what you have learnt and deciding where to go next. As an optional extra, I suggest that you create your own writing prompts for the next thirty days, rifting on the ones in this book.

DAY TWENTY-NINE

*R*eview what you've written so far. Make a note of anything that jumps out at you, anything you want to continue or that sparks off a story or poem or piece of nonfiction. Later on day twenty-nine, go through the exercises in this workbook and circle any you want to repeat, do differently or reinvent. Put a star next to the ones you really loved.

Now review at the times and places and energy levels you recorded next to your writing every day. When is the best time of day for you to write? When do you have most / least energy? Where do you feel most comfortable writing?

DAY THIRTY

G o on a walk. Make notes on the small details you observe. Later on day thirty, grab a notebook. Number 1 - 30 over a few pages. Add a writing prompt for each day. Use the ones you starred yesterday, and invent your own. Remember that you're aiming to use the prompts to get you to keep up your writing habit. Based on the review you carried out of time, place and energy-levels decide when and where you will write over the next thirty days. If you can't write each day, don't fret - schedule a *regular* writing time based on the time, place and energy-levels you've recorded. Establishing a habit is more important than trying to write every day.

*N*ext time you are on a train
Write about a train whilst on a train. Spend a few minutes on one or all of these short exercises.

1. Create the rhythm of the train in words.

2. Describe the rubbish people leave behind.

3. Describe the textures, colours and small details. What can you smell? What can you hear?

4. Make a list of the things you pass, or an aspect of them, like a colour.

5. Sketch the inside of buildings you can see from the windows, in words. Give a quick impression.

6. Note overheard dialogue, things people are doing, unusual possessions or items of clothing.

7. Any quirky characters? What is the atmosphere like? Impatient, relaxed, tired, exciting?

8. Sometimes one building, or tree, or item left out in a garden, or other feature, man-made or natural, will jump out at you as you pass it. Watch without writing for a while, then use whatever it is as a starting point.

9. Focus on one of the senses. Perhaps choose one you

wouldn't usually start with - taste or smell, for instance. Can you create a character who is experiencing that particular taste or smell (or whichever sense you have chosen)?

10. When you stop at a station, imagine the journey to that station. Is it remote or in the middle of a big city? Think of two characters, one who uses this station regularly and another who is there for the first time.

Now use your newly found writing habit to turn your train observations into a poem, short story, screenplay or stage play.

NOTES

NOTES

NOTES

NOTES

NOTES

NOTES

NOTES

NOTES

NOTES

NOTES

NOTES

NOTES

NOTES

NOTES

NOTES

NOTES

NOTES

NOTES

NOTES

NOTES

NOTES

NOTES

NOTES

NOTES

NOTES

NOTES

NOTES

NOTES

NOTES

ABOUT THE AUTHOR

Louise Tondeur published two novels with Headline Review: *The Water's Edge* and *The Haven Home for Delinquent Girls*. Then she travelled for a while, wrote a PhD, started a family, published short stories, poems and articles, and worked full-time as a university lecturer, all the time trying to find time to write amongst the hectic-ness of everyday life. She developed the Small Steps method to help her undergraduate students with time management skills, and to help herself carve out some writing time. Louise blogs about finding time to write on the Small Steps website at: www.smallstepsguide.co.uk Her author website is at: www.louisetondeur.co.uk Louise's first short story collection *Unusual Places* came out in 2018 with Cultured Llama.

facebook.com/louisetondeurwriter

twitter.com/LouiseTondeur

bookbub.com/profile/louise-tondeur

ALSO BY LOUISE TONDEUR

How to Write

How to Think Like a Writer

How to Write a Novel and Get It Published

CPSIA information can be obtained
at www.ICGtesting.com
Printed in the USA
LVHW080901071220
673521LV00043B/1399